Prince Harry and Meghan Markle

The inside story of the royal family, and the war with the Windsors

By

Danielle Dawson

Table of contents

Chapter 1: The history of their relationship; the timeline of the royal wedding

Prince Harry and Meghan Markle met back in 2016, and their lives have been a whirlwind ever since. From their secret courting to their fairytale wedding, a burgeoning family, and relocation across the pond, this is the history of their royal connection.

How they met

Harry and Markle initially made each other's acquaintance on a blind date in early July 2016.

News believes Harry's friend Violet von Westenholz is the one who introduced them, while some have believed it was fashion designer Mischa Nonoo.

Despite Prince Harry's worldwide reputation, Markle claims she didn't have a lot of preconceived preconceptions about who he was before they met. "Because I’m from the States, you don’t grow up with the same knowledge of the royal family," she stated.

"I didn’t know much about him, so the only thing that I had asked [our common acquaintance] when she said that she wanted to match us up, was, 'Well is he nice?' Cause if he wasn't nice, it simply didn’t seem like it would make sense."

The two hit it off instantly. "We met for a drink," recalled Markle, "and then I suppose pretty shortly into that we said, 'Well what are we doing tomorrow? We should meet again.'"

At the picture session on the Kensington Palace grounds after their engagement announcement, Harry was asked when he knew Markle was the one. He promptly answered, "the very first time we met."

Things proceeded swiftly from there. The duo went on a second date and Prince Harry then asked Markle to join him on a trip to Africa barely three or four weeks later. "I managed to convince her to come and join me in Botswana and we camped out with each other beneath the stars," he recalled, recounting the whirlwind affair.

"Then we were alone ourselves, which was vital to me to make sure that we had an opportunity to get to know each other."

The news goes out.

After four months of secret dating, the word eventually emerged on October 31, 2016, that Prince Harry was seeing an American actress. A source told that Harry is “happier than he’s been for many years” and is "besotted" with Markle.

According to Tina Brown, "a servant tip from the House of York" led to tabloids uncovering Harry and Meghan's connection.

On the same day, Markle uploaded a romantic picture on her Instagram of two bananas spooning, presumably hinting at the new love in her life.

Of this time, Markle later said: "We had a solid five, six months nearly with just seclusion, which was great."

Meghan meets the family.

In November 2016, there was an interview with Markle advertising her line for store Reitmans. In the conversation, she highlighted her cooperation with Reitmans, her charitable work with World Vision, and her plans for the holidays. Though she avoided any mention of Harry, she enthusiastically remarked, “So, my cup runneth over and I'm the happiest girl in the world!"

Around the same time, People claimed that Harry had previously introduced the actress to his father, Prince Charles.

Harry makes a statement in favor of Meghan.

Harry announced his connection with Markle in an official declaration on November 8, 2016. In the statement, Harry also asks the press and trolls on social media to halt the "wave of hatred and harassment" that had been aimed at his fiancée.

According to Harry, he has been engaged in "nightly legal battles" to stop the media from publishing disparaging claims about Markle and their relationship.

Prince Harry is anxious about Ms. Markle's safety and is profoundly upset that he has not been able to safeguard her. It is not proper that a few months into a relationship with him that Ms. Markle should be exposed to such a storm. He knows pundits will say this is ‘the price she has to pay and that ‘this is all part of the game’. He vehemently disagrees. This is not a game - it is her life and his.

Many felt that Markle would be prepared for the flood of attention since she had been in the public spotlight as an actress, but nothing could have prepared her for what was to follow.

"There was a notion that since I had worked in the entertainment world that this would be something I would be acquainted with," she added. "But I've never been part of tabloid culture. I've never engaged in pop culture to that degree and have lived a rather peaceful existence."

Her response, was to shut out the noise. "I believe we were simply struck so hard at the beginning with a lot of mistruths that I decided to not read anything, good or bad. It simply didn't make sense and instead we concentrated all of our energy only on fostering our love."

On November 18, she shared a Mahatma Gandhi quote on her Instagram, which many people interpreted as a response to Harry's statement on their relationship.

Even Prince William is obliged to weigh in.

On November 27, 2016, Prince William published a statement to clear up speculations that he was displeased with his brother's choice to come out about his relationship.

A section of the statement states, “The Duke of Cambridge understands the circumstances surrounding privacy and respects the necessity for Prince Harry to assist those closest to him."

Harry and Meghan continue to grow closer

In early December 2016, Markle is photographed in Toronto wearing a gold necklace featuring the letters “M” and “H.” Later that month, she and Harry are photographed together choosing out a 6-foot Christmas tree, and in London's West End holding hands on their way to attend the Tony award-winning production The Curious Incident of the Dog in the Nighttime.

The Queen approves

The Queen is “fully supportive” and another insider said that the Queen is “delighted to see Harry in a loving relationship.”

Markle talked about meeting the Queen during her interview. "It's fantastic to be able to meet her through his perspective, not only with his regard and respect for her as the queen but the love that he has for her as his grandmother. She's a great lady."

After spending Christmas with their families, the pair spends New Year's together in London.

Meghan's family makes the headlines.

Meghan’s half-brother Thomas Markle Jr. confesses that their father has been aware of Meghan's relationship since it started. In the interview, Thomas claims his father is, “pretty delighted about Harry and he’s proud of her."

At their engagement announcement, Markle disclosed that her father had talked with Harry numerous times, but he "hasn't been able to meet him just yet." As Thomas

Markle did not attend the royal wedding, and his relationship with his daughter is rather problematic, it's unknown in early 2022 whether he has ever met his royal son-in-law.

A romantic vacation to Norway

After spending New Year's in London, the couple goes on a romantic journey to Norway. This is the first time that the frequently incognito pair vacationed together and according to sources, Harry organized the romantic retreat so that the two could see the Northern Lights.

The pair stay with Harry's close friend, Inge Solheim, at his luxurious house in Tromsø, Norway.

Meghan meets Kate and Charlotte.

According to various sources, in early 2017 Harry brought his girlfriend to his sister-in-law Kate Middleton and Princess Charlotte in apartment 1A at Kensington Palace. According to the publication, Kate and Markle, "get on beautifully."

"She's been fantastic," Markle remarked of Duchess Kate. "Amazing," continued Harry. "As has William as well, you know, tremendous support."

Maintaining a long-distance relationship.

Though Markle shot her USA Network series Suits in Toronto, Canada, she and Harry are photographed in early February holding hands while leaving West London's Soho House.

According to a source, on-lookers at the member's only club said that the pair attempted to keep low-key by sitting in a secluded nook of the restaurant.

After a two-month absence from social media, Markle uploaded an Instagram photo on February 12 that wrote, "#NoBadEnergy."

In March, the pair flew together to Montego Bay, Jamaica to attend the wedding of Harry's boyhood friend Tom “Skippy” Inskip.

Markle is Harry's plus one at the wedding as the prince acts as one of the ceremony's 14 ushers. A source subsequently stated, that the two were exceedingly "joyful" throughout the wedding celebrations, and were very much in love.

In April, Harry traveled from England to spend the Easter holiday with Markle in Toronto.

Meghan's life starts to alter.

In April, Markle revealed that she will shut down her lifestyle website, The Tig, which she had launched three years earlier. In a statement released on both the Tig website and her Instagram, Markle said:

What started as a passion project (my little engine that could) developed into an extraordinary network of inspiration, support, fun, and frivolity. You’ve made my days brighter and filled my experience with so much pleasure. Keep finding those Tig moments of discovery, keep smiling and taking chances, and keep becoming the change you desire to see in the world."

Though it is reported that Markle shut down her passion project as a sacrifice to her royal romance, a source informed that the true reason was her hectic schedule, mixing charitable work with filming Suits.

The pair walks out.

Markle and Harry made their first public appearance as a couple (and shared a kiss) during the annual Audi Polo Challenge in Ascot, England.

As Harry competed in the sports, Markle, wearing a stunning blue dress and white jacket, cheered on her prince from the sidelines. The duo was then spotted indulging in some PDA off-site in the polo parking lot.

Markle was back in London in May for Pippa Middleton's wedding, arriving days ahead of the celebrations. The actress arrived at London's Heathrow Airport and was promptly brought to Kensington Palace. While Markle did not attend the wedding, she did go to the reception.

A huge birthday excursion

The pair journeyed to Africa in August 2017—a year after their first trip to the continent—for a romantic break in honor of Markle's 36th birthday. Throughout their three-week holiday, they visited Botswana and completed their journey at the magnificent Victoria Falls.

Meghan opens up

Markle talked publicly about her relationship for the first time in the October 2017 edition of Vanity Fair. "We're a couple. We're in love. I'm sure there will be a moment when we will have to come up and present ourselves and have tales to tell, but I think what people will realize is that this is our time," she adds in the cover story.

"This is for us. It's part of what makes it so unique, that's just ours. But we're happy. Personally, I enjoy a fantastic love tale."

That month, Markle also joined Prince Harry in an official royal appearance for the first time at the Invictus Games opening ceremony.

Throughout the games, cameras film the two holding hands at the Wheelchair Tennis semi-final and spending time with Markle's mother, Doria Ragland. The duo even share a romantic kiss during the closing ceremony.

At this stage, Harry had met Markle's mother numerous times. "Her mum's great," Harry stated during an interview.

Engaged!

After months of speculation, Prince Harry and Meghan Markle officially confirmed their engagement on November 27, 2017.

The pair is "thrilled and pleased" to be engaged, and commemorated the announcement with a party photoshoot and a formal interview.

Their engagement

In the months leading up to the wedding, Meghan has been exposed not just to the British public, but also to life as a working royal, as she attends official events with her fiancé Harry, all the while arranging the wedding of the year.

The wedding

Tens of millions of fans from across the globe tuned in to witness the pair wed at Windsor Castle on May 19.

They had high-profile guests like Oprah, David, and Victoria Beckham, and of course the royal family, but all eyes were on the bride, who donned a gorgeous Givenchy gown for the ceremony and a sleek halter

Stella McCartney dress for the reception at the Frogmore House.

In their official pictures, issued May 21, two days after the wedding, the couple seemed more in love than ever.

Harry and Meghan start a family!

On October 15, Kensington Palace announced that the Duke and Duchess of Sussex were expecting their first child. The statement came as the pair arrived in Australia for their first joint royal trip.

On May 6, 2019, Archie Harrison Mountbatten-Windsor came! The infant boy is now seventh in line for the throne and he is the Queen and Prince Philip's eighth great-grandson.

Harry's father, Prince Charles, and his stepmother, Camilla, Duchess of Cornwall declared that they are "delighted" with the royal baby's birth, as did the Queen, Duke of Edinburgh, and the Duke and Duchess of Cambridge.

The Sussexes pull back from their royal duties.

In January 2020, the Duke and Duchess of Sussex first made it known that they wanted to step back from their position as working royals. After a lengthy discussion, the Windsors decided to allow them to pursue their private business arrangements, provided that the Sussexes quit using the term "royal" in any professional branding.

Harry and Meghan formally moved to their new life at the end of March 2020, after returning shortly to the UK to conduct a last series of engagements. Subsequently, the two settled down with Archie in Santa Barbara, California.

They've undertaken a variety of initiatives in the meantime, including inking relationships with Netflix and Spotify and founding their new non-profit, Archewell.

A second baby Sussex is on the way!

On Valentine's Day of 2021, Harry and Meghan disclosed that they were expecting their second child. “We can confirm that Archie is going to be a big brother. The Duke and Duchess of Sussex are pleased to be expecting their second child,” a spokesman for the pair said. The pair also posted a lovely photo to commemorate the news.

The Queen assures the Sussexes won't return to the fold.

Nearly a year after formally moving out of the working royal positions, the Sussexes confirmed—along with Queen Elizabeth—that the shift was permanent. Buckingham Palace and the royal couple made identical statements on February 19, 2021, confirming the news.

The palace's announcement declared that Harry and Meghan would not be allowed to hold royal patronages and that Harry's military posts would also have to be returned.

It ended, "While everyone is grieved by their choice, The Duke and Duchess remain dearly loved members of the family."

For their part, Harry and Meghan highlighted in their statement that they “remain devoted to their duty and service" and "have pledged their continuous assistance to the organizations they have served regardless of formal role.” It said, “We may all live a life of service. Service is universal.”

The Duke and Duchess sat down for a momentous interview with Oprah.

According to Nielsen, 17.3 million people watched the highly anticipated talk live. In the two-hour interview, Meghan and Harry covered everything from their royal wedding to the sex of their second child (they're expecting a baby girl!) to their rationale for stepping aside as senior members of the royal family.

Lilibet 'Lili' Diana Mountbatten-Windsor is born.

On Sunday, June 6, Prince Harry and Meghan Markle announced that their daughter was delivered at The Santa Barbara Cottage Hospital in Santa Barbara, California on Friday, June 4 at 11:40 a.m.

The Duke and Duchess of Sussex named their second child after her great grandmother, Queen Elizabeth, whose family nickname is Lilibet, and her greatly cherished late grandmother the Princess of Wales.

They travel back to the UK.

Ahead of the Invictus Games, Harry and Meghan visited the Queen in Windsor, their first combined journey back to the UK since stepping aside from their royal obligations.

In June, they attended the Platinum Jubilee festivities with the rest of the royal family. As a spokeswoman stated in early May, “Prince Harry and Meghan, The Duke and Duchess of Sussex are pleased and privileged to attend The Queen’s Platinum Jubilee festivities in June with their children.”

They were sighted many times throughout the weekend, including at the National Service of Thanksgiving, which marked

Meghan's first royal function since stepping aside from her senior royal post.

Chapter 2: The hurting of the Royal family

Prince Harry and Meghan: Royal Family 'sad' as pair begin 'new chapter'

The Royal Family are "sad" by the Duke and Duchess of Sussex's decision they would step down as senior royals.

Prince Harry and Meghan did not contact any royal about preparing their statement, a palace insider informed.

Buckingham Palace was "blindsided", he added, since negotiations over their future had started but were in very early stages.

The palace acknowledged there were "complex challenges" to deal through.

In their statement on Wednesday, Harry and Meghan said they reached the decision "after many months of deliberation and internal conversations".

They claimed they plan "to stand aside as 'senior' members of the Royal Family, and seek to become financially independent".

They want to spend their time between the UK and North America, while "continuing to respect our responsibility to the Queen, the Commonwealth, and our patronages".

"This geographic balance will allow us to raise our baby with a respect for the royal tradition into which he was born, while also providing our family with the opportunity to concentrate on the next chapter," the pair stated.

Despite the couple's choice, Harry will remain sixth in line to the throne.

The duo was already planning to launch their own Sussex Royal charity, which they set up after divorcing from the Duke and Duchess of Cambridge's foundation in June last year.

The Sussexes' new organization is believed to be global, related to Africa and the US, rather than local - and will include a dedication to female empowerment.

It was disclosed in December the pair had applied to trademark their Sussex Royal brand across a series of things including books, calendars, clothes, charity fundraising, education, and social care services.

Why North America?

Meghan, of course, is American herself and has an especially tight bond with her mother who resides in California.

The pair have recently returned following a six-week hiatus from royal responsibilities, which they spent in Canada with their eight-month-old baby, Archie.

After returning to the UK, Harry, and Meghan, visited Canada's High Commission in London to thank the nation for hosting them and said the warmth and hospitality they experienced were "unbelievable".

Former actress Meghan lived and worked in Toronto for seven years during her time appearing in the famous US court show Suits.

She has previously talked of embracing the city as her second home after her hometown Los Angeles, and she has numerous Canadian pals.

Jessica Mulroney, a close friend of the duchess, tweeted a message on Instagram about a "strong lady" confronting a hardship.

The Canadian stylist and TV celebrity wrote: "A strong woman stares a problem in the eye and offers it a wink."

The couple's declaration raises various uncertainties concerning what their future royal positions may entail.

How will they become 'financially independent?

In stepping aside as senior royals, Harry and Meghan have stated they would no longer receive funds from the Sovereign Grant.

The pair stated this would make them "members of the Royal Family with financial freedom".

The Sovereign Grant is public money that pays for the expense of formal royal obligations, in return for the surrender by the Queen of the earnings from the Crown Estate.

The Queen's Sovereign Grant from the Treasury was £82m in 2018-19.

The pair claimed the Sovereign Grant pays for 5 percent of their official office from 2019, with the other 95 percent being supported by Prince Charles via his income from the Duchy of Cornwall.

Where do Prince Harry and Meghan receive their money?

Under existing laws, the duo claimed they are "prohibited from earning revenue in any manner", but in their future duties might join other title-holding royals in having full-time work.

The expenses of official abroad trips will be paid by the Sovereign Grant and payments from the host nation "where appropriate".

The pair are categorized as "internationally protected individuals", which means they must have armed protection supplied by the Metropolitan Police.

They will maintain Frogmore cottage, the Grade-2 listed house in Windsor that cost taxpayers £2.4m to repair, as their official residence so they have a "place to call home" in the UK.

What do commentators say?

Bryony Gordon, who knows and has interviewed the couple, indicated their choice may be connected to their mental health, after being a "punching bag" for a "misogynistic and racist" society.

In 2017, Ms. Gordon interviewed the prince for her Mad World podcast in which he disclosed he sought treatment while suffering in his late 20s to deal with the loss of his mother.

Speaking to Emma Barnett, she said: "Here is a man who every day has to live out the trauma that he experienced as a little boy when he had to walk behind her coffin at the age of 12 in front of the world, and I think if any of us were put in that situation we would find it incredibly triggering."

She claimed the pair had become a "punching bag for a society that is still kind of terribly sexist and racist" and they were "entitled" to "do what is best" for their family's mental health.

She expects the pair will go on precisely as before "but simply for free" since they're "weary of the attention" that comes with collecting public money.

Royal analyst Penny Junor claimed the couple's behaviors were reminiscent of those of Harry's mother, Diana, Princess of Wales. The allegation that they had not contacted other royals before making their statement was "beyond absurd".

She said: "It has echoes of Diana when she abruptly declared after her separation [from Charles] that she was stepping down from 50 of her organizations without consulting anyone.

"The difficulty is that they are not working for themselves, they are working for a family company and to be making pronouncements of this like without consultation is beyond strange."

Graham Smith, a spokesperson for Republic, which fights for an elected head of state, said Harry and Meghan's choice "raises doubts about the monarchy's future" and would force taxpayers to wonder how the couple's increased security and abroad lifestyle will be paid.

"To claim that they're not already financially independent is vulgar and reflects a feeling of self-entitlement and a lack of self-awareness that is prevalent among royals," he added.

"This truly is trying to have your cake and eat it. They have indicated they would dip in and out of royal responsibilities as it suits them but won't stop receiving public money until they discover other means of revenue."

There are considerably more questions than answers. What will their new role be? Where will they reside, and who will pay for it? What connection will they have with the rest of the Royal Family?

And there's the institutional issue - what does this signify for the Royal Family?

But Harry and Meghan touched individuals that earlier royals didn't. They were part of the reinvention and renewal of the institution.

We're now in wait-and-see mode as to whether this new model of being a royal can succeed - or whether this is truly a staging station for them to depart the Royal Family.

Was it a surprise?

Signs the pair were dissatisfied with their royal life had been clear for some months.

In October last year, the Duchess of Sussex initiated legal action against the Mail on a claim that it improperly published one of her private letters. The publication stands by its narrative.

At the time, Prince Harry stated his wife had "become one of the latest victims of a British tabloid press" amid a "ruthless campaign" of "relentless misinformation".

"Though we have continued to put on a brave front... I cannot begin to convey how hard it has been," he added.

In an ITV documentary last year, Meghan, who was born in the US, characterized parenting as a "battle" owing to significant attention from tabloids. "Not many people have inquired whether I'm OK," she remarked.

Shadow health secretary Jonathan Ashworth said the press should "leave Harry and Meghan alone" in the aftermath of their choice.

The Labour MP for Leicester South offered sympathy for the marriage, saying that the duchess had experienced "appalling" abuse and that she "deserves a break".

The royal couple declared they will be adopting a "revised media strategy" from the spring.

As part of the new approach, detailed on their website, they will "connect with grassroots media groups and young, up-and-coming journalists".

They will also opt out of the so-called royal rota system, where journalists and media representatives are granted exclusive access to cover royal events on the premise they share the information they obtain.

"The existing structure precedes the enormous shift of news reporting in the digital era," the pair stated.

The National Union of Journalists condemned the measures, saying the action appeared to attempt to "block the media from working and undermining the capacity of journalists to perform their duties, which is utterly unacceptable".

Harry is sixth in line to the throne - following Prince Charles, Prince William, and his three children.

Chapter 3: What happens next? What we know so far

The Duke and Duchess of Sussex are stepping aside from royal responsibilities and will spend their time between the UK and North America, Buckingham Palace has announced.

They will no longer use their HRH titles and will cease receiving public cash for royal tasks under the "new arrangement".

The couple, who have a young boy, Archie, had previously claimed they hoped to carve out a "progressive new position" in the Royal Family and intended to "fight to become financially independent".

What would the 'next chapter' look like?

Following the announcement from the Queen, a supplementary statement from

Buckingham Palace stated the pair were thankful to the queen and the Royal Family for their support as they "embark on the next chapter of their life".

It added they knew they are "obliged to stand aside from royal obligations, including formal military postings".

The pair will continue to retain their private patronages and relationships "with the Queen's permission", the statement stated.

Prince Harry and Meghan announced earlier they want to start a new "charitable organization".

Exactly where and exactly what is unknown since the pair have not yet expanded on how they envision their new job.

However, their new organization is anticipated to be worldwide in scope, with part of the emphasis likely to be on the US and Africa.

On the pair's first official foreign visit last year with their baby, Archie, the Duchess of Sussex told young girls in a poor section of South Africa that she was with them "as a lady of color and as your sister".

Prince Harry has talked of his passion for Africa, describing the continent as a location "where I feel more like myself than anyplace else in the world".

The couple's charitable activity is also expected to include a dedication to female empowerment, a topic on which Meghan has openly committed to "shine a light".

How will they afford their new life?

The Duke and Duchess of Sussex will not receive taxpayer funding for royal obligations.

They have declared their objective is to "work to become financially independent".

David McClure, the author of a book on how royals have gained and spent their riches, said they already had their own money and might generate more from TV in the future.

Meghan was allegedly paid $50,000 (£38,400) for every episode of the TV drama Suits. While she is no longer a professional actor she will earn some money anytime the episode is rerun.

Currently, the duke and duchess's expenditures - such as living costs, travel, and wardrobe - are funded by Harry's father for their job as working royals, representing the Queen.

The Prince of Wales pays his sons and their families with revenue from the Duchy of Cornwall.

Where will they be based?

They aim to split their time between the UK and North America.

They just moved into their new house - Frogmore Cottage in Windsor, Berkshire - in April ahead of the birth of their baby. The anticipated cost to the taxpayer of upgrades to it is roughly £2.4m.

Buckingham Palace stated in a statement the pair had "expressed their intention to refund Sovereign Grant expenses" for the restoration of Frogmore Cottage.

It will remain their UK family home, the palace said.

Harry and Meghan enjoyed an extended vacation from royal obligations during Christmas, including time spent in the Canadian state of British Columbia.

While playing in the US program Suits, Toronto became an adopted city for Meghan. It is home to her pals, Jessica and Ben Mulroney, the city's "most polished power couple", according to Toronto Life magazine.

It is expected that the family would spend time in Meghan's US country too As her mother, Doria Ragland, resides in California.

Her father, Thomas Markle, with whom Meghan has limited contact, resides in Mexico.

What's driving the decision?

Many months of contemplation and internal debates, they stated.

In October, the public got a look inside the couple's worldview in an ITV documentary taped on a trip to Africa.

The Duchess of Sussex confessed adapting to royal life had been "challenging" and she had not been prepared for the severity of the media scrutiny, despite warnings from her British friends that the tabloids might "destroy" her life.

Asked if she was coping, Meghan, a new mother, replied: "I have said for a long time to H - that is what I call him - it's not enough to simply endure anything, it's not the objective of life. You have got to flourish."

Prince Harry has characterized his mental health and the way he deals with the stresses of his life as a subject of "continuous management".

At the moment, an uninhibited Harry said: "I lost my mother and now I witness my wife falling prey to the same terrible forces."

Referring to his mother, Diana, Princess of Wales' tragic death in 1997, he said: "I've seen what happens when someone I love gets commoditized to the extent where they are no longer regarded or recognized as a genuine person."

The duke said he and Meghan had planned to continue serving the Queen, but without public financing. "Unfortunately, it wasn't doable," he remarked.

In his address, shared on the couple's Instagram account, Prince Harry also talked of his "deep grief" about his and Meghan's new connection with the Royal Family.

"The choice that I have taken for my wife and me to step back is not one I made lightly," he stated.

Following the announcement from the Queen that the couple were stepping down from royal responsibilities and can no longer officially represent the Queen, Buckingham Palace stated the Sussexes have made clear that everything they do would "continue to respect the principles of Her Majesty".

While no information has been released concerning security plans for the newlyweds, the statement claimed: that "there are well-established and impartial systems to identify the necessity for publicly-funded protection".

Under a header asking what Harry and Meghan's view is on the media in general, the pair stated they believe in a "free, powerful and open media" that "upholds truth and supports openness, diversity, and tolerance".

"Their Royal Highnesses recognize that their roles as members of the Royal Family are subject to interest, and they welcome accurate and honest media reporting as well as being held to account if appropriate. Equally, like every member of society, they also value privacy as individuals and as a family."

The pair said they will continue to use social media, particularly their Instagram account which has 10.1m followers, to "personally share events in their life directly with members of the public".

Chapter 4: The conflict with the Windsors

Prince Harry and Meghan Markle were not invited to Balmoral for Queen's retreat

There'll be no wafts of Scottish heather and brisk treks for Prince Harry and Meghan Markle since they are not on the Balmoral summer visitor list.

Despite rumors the Duke and Duchess of Sussex were invited to join Queen Elizabeth on her annual summer getaway in the highlands, we're informed there was no such request.

Servants at the 96-year-old monarch's Scottish estate had been informed to anticipate a full list of royals, including "Harry, Meghan and their children Archie and Lilibet."

However, many sources confirmed that the Sussexes would not be traveling to see Harry's grandma.

The pair will remain in the US ahead of the release of Harry's much-anticipated book this autumn.

Harry, 37, and Markle, 40, last met the Queen in June when they went to the UK to celebrate her Platinum Jubilee. There, they presented newborn daughter Lilibet — called Lili — to the monarch for the first time.

Queen Elizabeth last visited the Sussexes in June.

Although they were not allowed onto the balcony at Buckingham Palace, the Sussexes — sans children — then attended the Trooping the Colour event and a Service of Thanksgiving at St Paul's Cathedral.

However, they did not spend any private time with Harry's brother, Prince William, his wife Kate Middleton, and their three children. Although they invited them to Lilibet's first birthday at their UK residence, Frogmore Cottage, they were in Wales on official business.

They did manage to present Lilibet to her grandpa, Prince Charles, in an "emotional" encounter, sources close to the heir to the throne subsequently stated.

The Queen was observed in Scotland this week and will spend the months of August and September at her highland hideaway, where she will be joined by other family members, including William, Kate, and their kids, Prince George, 9, Princess Charlotte, 7, and Prince Louis, 4.

Chapter 5: Astonishing Facts about their daughter Lilibet

Prince Harry and Meghan Markle's baby Lilibet Diana: 7 amazing facts

Did you know?

Prince Harry and Meghan Markle's daughter Lilibet Diana was born on 4 June 2021, more than two years after her brother Archie. Now the royal tot turns one – we take a look at seven startling things you may not know about her...

Lilibet is named after her grandma and great grandmother

In 2021, the couple welcomed Lilibet "Lili" Diana Mountbatten-Windsor into the family. Explaining their choice of name, they added: "Lili is named after her great-grandmother, Her Majesty The Queen, whose family nickname is Lilibet.

"Her middle name, Diana, was chosen to commemorate her adored late grandmother, The Princess of Wales."

The moniker 'Lilibet' is claimed to have come about because a young Queen, then Princess Elizabeth, couldn't pronounce her name so she called herself 'Lilibet' instead.

Lilibet has the same middle name as her cousin

Lilibet shares the middle name Diana with her cousin, Princess Charlotte, who is the daughter of Prince William and the Duchess of Cambridge.

Lilibet was born in a foreign nation to her sibling

The Duchess of Sussex gave birth to her daughter in the US at Santa Barbara Cottage Hospital, whilst her son Archie was delivered in the UK, at the Portland Hospital in London. This wasn't necessarily an intentional decision, merely down to where the couple was living at the time.

Lilibet's parents realized they were carrying a daughter

Unlike with baby Archie, Prince Harry and Meghan Markle opted to find out whether they were expecting a boy or girl while Meghan was pregnant with Lilibet. So, they may have had the charming name in mind for a while ahead of her birth.

Lilibet is eight in line to the throne

The official royal website explains that Miss Lilibet Mountbatten-Windsor is eight in line to the throne, just below her brother Archie but above her great uncle Prince Andrew.

This comes after the rules changed to allow female counterparts to be considered in lineage.

Lilibet was nearly one when she met the Queen for the first time

When Prince Harry and Meghan Markle were in the UK for the Queen's Platinum Jubilee, they brought their daughter Lilibet to visit Her Majesty for the first time. It was an off-camera private encounter for the family to enjoy away from the media.

Lilibet has the same star sign as Prince Philip

Lilibet was born on 4 June which makes her a Gemini, which is the same star sign as the late Prince Philip, who is her great grandfather who celebrated his birthday on 10 June. The astrological charts identify Geminis as "kind, loving, inquiring and flexible".

Printed in Great Britain
by Amazon